The Humane Society of the United States

Hope

Written by: Randy Houk

Illustrated by: Walt Sturrock

for Blaine and Taylor Hudson,
who bring me joy and laughter
~ Randy Houk

for my son Sean, who
has inspired me in ways
beyond measure
~ Walt Sturrock

THE
BENEFACTORY

2

$\mathcal{H}$ope was born one summer morn.
No one clapped, or blew a horn.
She was just another pig -
Pinkish-white, and not so big.
She was barely two pounds weight,
Smallest of the littermates.

Luckily, there were just ten
Piglets in the farrow pen.
Hope was last in line to nurse.
Larger piglets pushed in first.
Stronger piglets claimed the front.
Hope was just a little runt.

Hope got lots of milk that day.
She began to romp and play,
Bumping, squealing with her brothers,
Tumbling, grunting with the others,
Rooting through the bed of hay,
Climbing, while her mother lay.

Late at night the piglets sleep
Piled up in a velvet heap.
There's a light to give them heat
And by nature, pigs are neat.
Even newborn piglets try:
They like their nest clean and dry.
(Only when it's hot would they
Wallow in the mud all day.
That's because a pig can't sweat:
Pigs stay cool in mud that's wet.)

*H*ope would never miss a feed.
She grew quickly, like a weed.
Soon she matched the others' weight
Though she'd started small and late.

Born inside a factory farm,
At best, Hope was safe from harm.
When Hope reached three weeks of age,
She was put into a cage.
Taken from her loving mother,
With her sisters, with her brothers.

Hope grew quickly, Hope grew fast.
Hope was fed a lot of mash,
Soybean mix, and scraps and whey,
Many feedings every day.

*D*ark and cramped inside the crate,
For three months the piglets wait.
Here they could not turn around,
Root for acorns in the ground.

In the crate, the floor was wire,
Not the floor pigs' hooves require.
With the piglets jammed in close,
Piglets often caught their toes.

No one heard Hope's painful squeal.
No one cared what Hope might feel.
When a worker finally came,
Poor Hope's leg was bent and lame.

Though he got her toes set free,
No one brought a vet to see.
No one cared, for soon she would
Grow enough to sell for food.

She was meant to gain more weight,
But the more she gained and ate,
All the more her leg grew lame,
From the weight upon her frame.
And, before she got much older,
That poor bent leg could not hold her.
She would try to walk, and fall.
Soon she couldn't walk at all.

"Toss her out," a worker spat.
"We can't sell a pig like that."
In a dumpster Hope was tossed.
She lay thinking all was lost.

Lying in the dark one day,
Watching shadows slip away,
Hope heard noises just outside.
Hope heard noises, and she cried.

"Something's in there," someone said.
"In the dumpster, left for dead.
Open up the lid – be quick.
It sounds dreadful. It sounds sick."

Up the lid flew, and the light
Made Hope blink, it was so bright.
Then she felt a gentle hand.
"Oh, how awful," said a man.
"She's alive," a woman said.
"It's a wonder she's not dead.
You can see her leg's not right.
She's a pretty sorry sight."

"Can we keep her?" said the voice.
"Have we really got a choice?
Leg or no, she can't stay here,
Barely hanging on – that's clear.
She needs food, she needs a vet.
Maybe we'll save that leg yet."

They were careful, they were kind.
In the truck, Hope rode behind.
In a blanket she was rolled,
Sheltered from the damp and cold.
To a farm in New York state,
That truck drove, and got there late.

In a barn, in soft, dry hay,
Under heat lamps, Hope soon lay.
Hope was given food to eat,
Warm mash, for a special treat.
She was cleaned and then rubbed dry.
She gave one long, grateful sigh.

"She'll be fine," the kind man said.
"Leave her, Lorri. Go to bed."
"Okay, Gene, but you come too.
You've done all there is to do."

Hope felt peaceful, warm and cozy.
Hope felt safe and full and dozey.
Hope felt something kind of bump
Up against her soft, pink rump.
Lifting up her head, she saw
There beside her, in the straw,
Quite a handsome, spotted pig,
Gray and white and not so big.

21

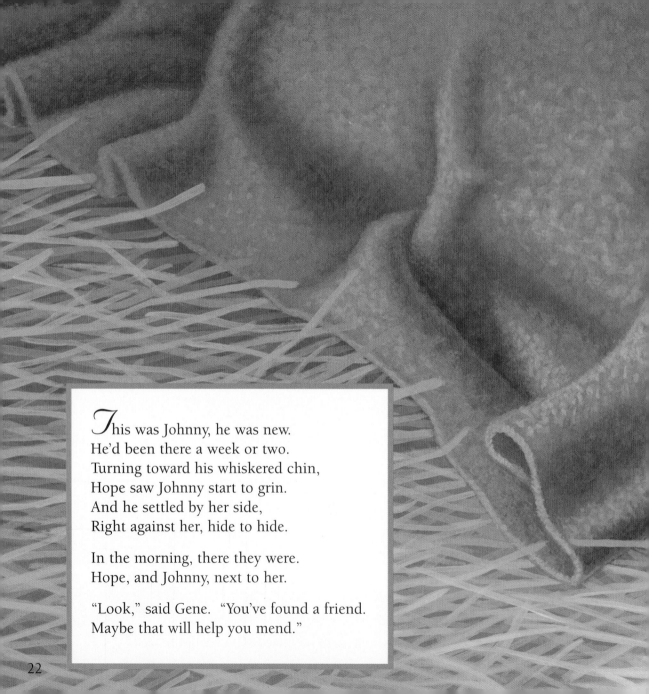

This was Johnny, he was new.
He'd been there a week or two.
Turning toward his whiskered chin,
Hope saw Johnny start to grin.
And he settled by her side,
Right against her, hide to hide.

In the morning, there they were.
Hope, and Johnny, next to her.

"Look," said Gene. "You've found a friend.
Maybe that will help you mend."

Later on, the vet inspected
Hope, and said, "This leg's infected.
I'm afraid it's gone too long.
This leg always will be wrong.
Keep an eye on her, you two.
See what she can learn to do.
She seems happy. Look at her.
If she were a cat, she'd purr."

*H*ope felt safe, she liked this place:
You could see it on her face.
Johnny rubbed against her hide.
Johnny wouldn't leave her side.
Hope was smiling. You could tell
She felt happy. She felt well.

"Maybe she can learn to cope,"
Lorri said. "Let's name her 'Hope'."

Hope's still at the Sanctuary.
She can't walk, but still she's merry.
She can kind of scoot around,
Pull her bad leg on the ground.
Johnny's with her every day.
She's his mate for life, they say.

28

Hope's now a nine-hundred pounder.
She's glad Gene and Lorri found her.
Children come from near and far,
Come in bus and come in car.
They see sheep, and lambs and cows.
They see rabbits, they see sows;
Turkeys, goats and chickens too,
Pigs that fetch, and come to you;
Pigs as smart as any dog.
(No dog's smarter than a hog.)

They pat Johnny, they pat Hope.
They can tell she's learned to cope.
They hear Gene and Lorri tell
How to treat farm creatures well.

If you think you'd like to see
How farm animals can be,
When they're loved and kept with care,
The Farm Sanctuary's there,
Thirty miles from Watkins Glen.
Go and see. You'll make a friend.

Glossary

littermates	all the pigs born to one sow (mother pig) at one time
farrow pen	a pen where a sow has her litter (baby piglets)
nurse	drink milk from the mother
runt	the smallest in a litter
velvet	a very soft, fuzzy cloth
vet	a doctor for animals
dumpster	a bin where garbage is thrown
grateful	thankful
rump	rear end, hip
cope	get along okay, make things work out

The real Hope and Johnny

Farm Sanctuary operates public shelters for victims of "food animal" production. Since co-founders Gene and Lorri Bauston formed the orgnization in 1986, Farm Sanctuary has rescued and provided life-long care for hundreds of animals. Hope's story is based on several rescue efforts. For more information on tours, campaigns and shelter programs, please contact:

Farm Sanctuary – East
P.O. Box 150
Watkins Glen, NY 14891
(607) 583-2225

Farm Sanctuary – West
P.O. Box 1065
Orlando, CA 95963
(916) 865-4617

The Humane Society of the U.S., a nonprofit organization founded in 1954, and with a constituency of over two million persons, is dedicated to speaking for animals, who cannot speak for themselves. The HSUS is devoted to making the world safe for animals through legal, educational, legislative and investigative means. The HSUS believes that humans have a moral obligation to protect other species with which we share the Earth. Co-sponsorship of this book by The Humane Society of the United States does not imply any partnership, joint venture, or other direct affiliation between The HSUS and Farm Sanctuary. For information on The HSUS, call: (202) 452-1100.

Text and Illustrations
Copyright © 1995
by Randy Houk

Printed by
Allied Printing Services, Inc.
Designed by
Anita Soos Design, Inc.

THE BENEFACTORY

Published by The Benefactory, Inc.
One Post Road, Fairfield, CT 06430
The Benefactory produces books, tapes, and toys that foster animal protection and environmental preservation.
Call: 203-255-7744

ISBN 1-882728-34-3
Printed in the U.S.A.
10 9 8 7 6 5 4 3 2 1